Farsley Omnibus Company and Kippax & District Motor Co. Ltd:
Leeds' Wallace Arnold stage bus companies

Stuart Emmett

This book concentrates on the urban operators of the Farsley Omnibus Company and Kippax & District of Leeds. Wallace Arnold also had another stage bus company, the rural country bus service of Hardwicks Motor Services from Ebberston to Scarborough. To put all of Wallace Arnold's stage operations into perspective, the following is a summary from 1966:

- Hardwicks' hourly service was effectively one main 15-mile rural route from Scarborough to Ebberston and had three double-deckers and four single-deckers. They carried up to 480,000 passengers per year and operated from 1952 to 1987.

- Farsley Omnibus Co. Ltd., Richardshaw Lane, Stanningley. Farsley OC had a 5-mile intensive 15/30 min headway urban route between Pudsey to Horsforth via Farsley and Rodley on the western outskirts of Leeds. They had six double-deckers, carrying up to 2.3m passengers per year, and operated from 1952 to 1968.

- Kippax and District Motor Co. Ltd., Butt Hill, Kippax, ran from Leeds to Ledston Luck, via Cross Gates, Garforth and Kippax on the Eastern outskirts of Leeds. The hourly service operated with six double-deckers carrying up to 1.4m passengers per year on the 11-mile route, and operated from 1956 to 1968.

So, with that as background, let us examine here, in more detail, the Farsley and Kippax operations. Hardwicks is covered by another book in this series.

Text © Stuart Emmett, 2020.
First published in the United Kingdom, 2020,
by Stenlake Publishing Ltd.,
54-58 Mill Square,
Catrine, Ayrshire,
KA5 6RD

Telephone: 01290 551122
www.stenlake.co.uk

ISBN 9781840338584

Printed by P2D,
1 Newlands Road,
Westoning,
MK45 5LD

The publishers regret that they cannot supply copies of any pictures featured in this book.

Sources

J.B. Parkin, "The End of Kippax and Farsley", *Buses Magazine*, August 1969.
J. Soper, *Leeds Transport, Volume 4, 1953 to 1974*, Leeds Transport Historical Society (LTHS), 2007.
Farsley Omnibus Co. Ltd. 1920-1968, History and Fleet List, Local Transport History Society, May 2015.
Kippax and District Motor Co. Ltd., 1924-1968, History and Fleet List, Local Transport History Society, 2015.
Wallace Arnold Tours Limited, Part 1 and 2 – 1919 to 1979, PSV Circle/Omnibus Society, Fleet History PB15/16, May and July 1979.

Acknowledgements

Unless stated below, the pictures are from my own collection that is made up of our family pictures and other unknown sources. For the latter, the original photographer cannot be traced, I offer my apologies to them for the lack of accreditation and would be pleased to be able to correct this in future editions.

John Cockshott Archive from the Transport Library: pages 11 (lower), 14 (lower), 15 (lower), 19, 20 (lower), 21 (upper).
Paul Heywood: page 35.
Huddersfield Passenger Transport Group: page 34.
John Kaye: pages 20 (upper), 39 (upper).
Leeds Transport Historical Society: pages 14 (upper), 17, 22 (lower), 29, 30, 33, 38, 41, 44 (lower), 45.
PM Photography: pages 3, 9, 10, 12, 13, 16, 23 (lower), 26.
Travel Lens Photographic: pages 23 (upper), 25, 27 (both), 40, 43 (lower), 46.

The typical Farsley bus, a rebodied Daimler CVD6 with Roe H61R body with the chassis donor a former Wallace Arnold 1949 half cab body coach. MUB433's original Wilks and Meade body had been replaced in 1954 by a Plaxton FC33F body and then in January 1957 with this Roe body. It is on the single 5-mile route from Horsforth to Pudsey and is halfway there at Rodley, in the Aire Valley, where it is turning up to Bagley Lane to Farsley for Stanningley and Pudsey.

The Farsley Route and its History

For those not familiar with the area, Pudsey is a market town in West Yorkshire which was incorporated into the City of Leeds metropolitan borough in 1974. The town was famous in the 18th and 19th centuries for wool manufacture and during the Industrial Revolution, Pudsey was one of the most polluted areas of the UK due to its position midway between the two coal smoke industrial cities of Leeds and Bradford. With a population of around 23,000, it is perhaps best-known today for being the birthplace of "Pudsey Bear", the BBC mascot for the fundraising programme "Children in Need", (Pudsey Bear's logo designer's grandfather was, at the time, the mayor at Pudsey).

Pudsey is around 200 feet above sea level and is across the Aire Valley from Horsforth that is around 150 feet with Rodley about halfway between them. Coming from Pudsey to Rodley involves passing through Farsley which was also a centre for wool processing. Rodley was the home of Thomas Smith's Steam Crane works, that was taken over by various companies along with their next door neighbours, Joseph Booth, who also made cranes. Whilst Booth's works has subsequently been demolished and redeveloped with housing, the former Thomas Smith works building survived, and is now the home for several small engineering companies.

Horsforth has a history of producing high quality stone from its quarries and has provided stone for Kirkstall Abbey, Scarborough seafront as well as exporting sandstone from its Golden Bank Quarry. As with Pudsey it has a history in the textile trade and today is also at the end of the runway for the Leeds Bradford International Airport.

Pudsey, Farsley, Rodley and Horsforth are all now dormitory towns for Leeds, currently the second largest financial centre outside of London.

Farsley Omnibus

The forerunners of the Farsley Omnibus Co. Ltd commenced trading in the early 1920s under the ownership of E&W Lawson, and were based in a garage in Town Street, Stanningley. The original route was the 2 miles between Stanningley and Rodley, via Farsley.

In April 1927 it was purchased by Maurice Greenwood, who renamed the business the Farsley Omnibus Company (FOC) and controlled the company for the next 25 years. It never went beyond having a single route, although the route was later extended from each terminus.

In 1933 an application was made to extend north from Rodley to Horsforth (Old Ball Hotel), using the newly-built Leeds Ring Road. Following a lengthy battle with the Traffic Commissioners, the application was granted with a curtailment in Horsforth to The Green. It began in April 1934, running from Sunfield, opposite to the bottom of Richardshaw Lane in Stanningley. Greenwood was not, however, finished and in 1937, despite objections from Leeds Corporation Transport, he got permission to extend south from Stanningley to Pudsey Town Hall in direct competition with the Leeds trams, although with restrictions placed on the carriage of passengers on the section between Stanningley and Pudsey.

With the advent of the Second World War in 1939, these restrictions were removed as an emergency measure and then were never re-imposed in peacetime and the unrestricted carriage of passengers then continued.

The route was again extended in June 1949 to the earlier requested Horsforth Old Ball Hotel, where it met the Ledgard's Leeds via Hawksworth Road to Horsforth service and the joint Ledgard/West Yorkshire route from Rawdon to Leeds. Additionally, once a day, West Yorkshire ran from Cookridge, (4 minutes beyond the Old Ball to the Holt Lane police box), to Bradford via Calverley and Greengates. This ran once in the morning. with an evening return and was later cut back from Cookridge to Horsforth Railway Station.

The Farsley route was intensive with a 15 or 20 minute headway needing four or three buses respectively. The journey from Pudsey to the Old Ball took 25 minutes for the 5.03 miles with some shorts to Farsley (9 minutes) and from Stanningley to Rodley (7 minutes). On Sundays one bus was enough for the 60 minute morning headway, until the 20 minute headway started at 1300 hours.

Affectionately known as the "Farsley Fliers", they had many regular passengers with a village bus atmosphere where most passengers knew each other. However, in 1952 Mr. Greenwood said the buses were no longer paying and on 1st October that year, he sold the business to Barr & Wallace Arnold Trust of Leeds. Farsley continued to be operated as a subsidiary with the existing red and cream livery retained. The Farsley garage at Town Street, Stanningley was, however, not taken over and was sold to a haulage contractor, the Farsley fleet being moved to the existing Wallace Arnold garage at 63, Richardshaw Lane, Pudsey.

The route had a few developments, and these are mentioned below. A full route map is shown and shows the route numbers used later by Leeds CT; the map is used courtesy of the Leeds Transport Historical Society.

- In April 1954 some peak-hour extras were diverted at Farsley from the main route via Coal Hill Lane and Rodley Town Street to serve the Smith Crane Works at Rodley.

- On October 13th 1956 at certain times, the route was extended by 0.8 of a mile from Horsforth Old Ball via the railway station into Tinshill. It was worked exclusively by single-deckers because of a weight restriction on the bridge over the railway at Horsforth.

- Also, on 13th October 1956 the Farsley Pudsey terminus moved from Robin Lane to the new bus station about 50 yards away.

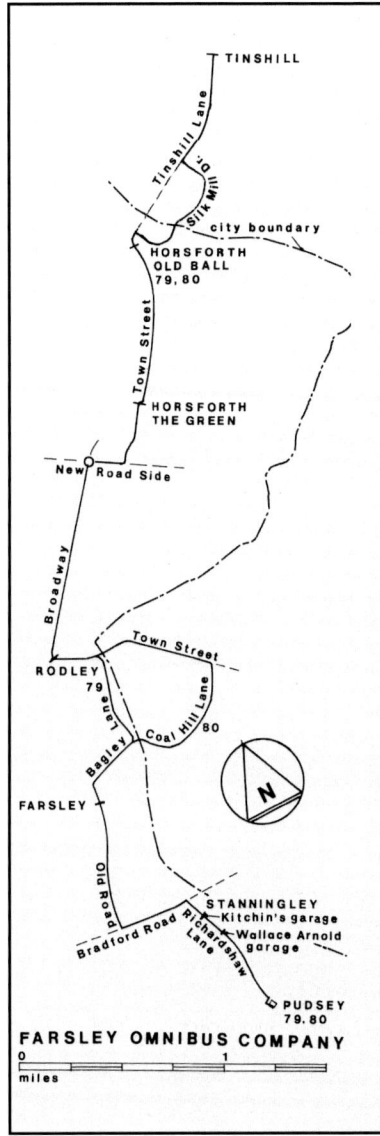

- In January 1959, after Wallace Arnold Tours (WAT) acquired the Pudsey coach fleet of J.W. Kitchen & Sons, the Farsley fleet was re-housed in Kitchen's former Cavendish Garage premises, also in Richardshaw Lane, a little further down from the Wallace Arnold garage, which then was closed. Kitchens had also once operated a stage route from Pudsey to Calverley and this route, along with their four vehicle bus fleet, had been sold to Ledgards in April 1957.

- From 21st August 1960, due to a decline in passenger traffic, the service frequency in the evenings and on Sundays was reduced from every 20 minutes to half-hourly.

- On 30th October 1960 Leeds Corporation Transport started their route 9 around the Ring Road every two hours, and every hour at peak time; this shared the Farsley route between Rodley roundabout and the Horsforth roundabout.

- Finally, on 10th October 1967 British Railways imposed a 2-ton weight limit on the bridge at Horsforth Station, so the Tinshill extension was suspended. It was reintroduced on 9th September 1968, after the Leeds takeover and following a rebuilding of the bridge.

By February 1967 the route was mainly one-man operated using three single-deckers (9206/7 NW and 833KUA), with double-deckers on the weekday peak periods. However, on Saturdays, double-deckers were often used because of the volume of traffic and the single-deckers were then regularly employed on WAT excursions, especially during the main summer coaching season.

Ready for excursion work, Farsley 833KUA is outside WAT's Feather Brothers office on Morley Street, Bradford.

The Fleet

The early livery of red and cream remained basically unaltered throughout the life of the undertaking and although fleet numbers were later used by the Greenwood owned FOC, not all vehicles carried them. The fleet inherited by WAT was a mixture of new and second-hand single-deckers, but the only vehicles retained after the take-over were four 1947/1948 Roe B35F bodied Daimler CVD6s.

Fleet details are in a fleet list available on request and this gives fuller details of the complexity of buses used and also the many Wallace Arnold coaches loaned. The following provides an overview of the fleet policy:

In the take-over, the four old FOC Leyland and Daimlers from the 1930s went, and were replaced by four coaches loaned from the Wallace Arnold fleet. These were a mixed bag of WAT 1937/38 Leyland TS7/8s, that had been involved in the large-scale post-war WAT rebuilding/bodying programme and now had Burlingham bodies.

These four loaned coaches stayed on for two years when another four WAT coaches replaced them in 1954, all 1949 Daimlers with bodies from the WAT-owned Wilks and Meade. They turned out to be robust vehicles as in 1956 they were rebodied with Roe double-deck bodies. These worked until the late 1960s, either with Farsley or the associated Hardwicks and Kippax fleets.

Whilst the Daimlers were away being rebodied, three more coaches came on loan from WAT, again Daimlers but this time from 1947 and whilst originally, they also had Wilks and Meade bodies, these three were rebodied in late 1952 with Plaxton full front bodies from other WAT coaches. One of them in 1957 (KUM849) was also, later, rebodied by Roe as a double-decker.

In 1954 the first double-deck vehicle was added to the fleet. This was DUB926, an ex-Leeds Corporation Leyland TD4, and came via another Wallace Arnold subsidiary, Hardwicks of Scarborough. At the time Horsforth Urban District Council objected to the running of double-deckers in Town Street, Horsforth and initially DUB926 was restricted to the Pudsey to Rodley section of the route. However, by April 1955, the objections had been dropped and the vehicle could now work the full route to the Old Ball Hotel in Horsforth.

In October 1955, when three of the former WAT Wilks and Meade C33F-bodied Daimler CVD6 coaches had received new double-deck bodies by Roe and entered service, double-deck vehicles began to predominate in the fleet for the first time. Another double-decker formerly with Leeds Corporation came in from Hardwicks for a few months before returning to WAT and was replaced at Farsley, by another Roe-rebodied Daimler.

The late 1956 single-deck requirement for operation over the railway bridge to Tinshill had been originally worked by two of the original Farsley Daimler/Roe single-deckers. However, after two months these went to WAT Leeds for contract work and were replaced by two WAT AEC Regal/Bellhouse Hartwell coaches in 1957. In 1958 these were replaced by two more WAT AEC Reliance coaches, one with a Plaxton Consort body, the other one being a Burlingham Seagull; both had central entrances. Then in 1961 came a WAT Leyland Tiger Cub with Burlingham Seagull body which stayed until 1965.

A 36ft AEC Reliance demonstrator (327NMP) was on loan in May/June 1962 and was probably an experiment in high capacity single-deck bus operation, as in 1964 a new Leyland with Plaxton Highway body entered the fleet and joined a new Leyland PD3 with Roe body from 1963 (the company's first 30ft double-decker). Another PD3 came in 1966 and also two Kippax vehicles are recorded as assisting at Farsley during 1965/1966.

Also entering the fleet were two former WAT AEC Reliance's with Plaxton Panorama I bodies in 1965 and 1967, the first one replacing the earlier Burlingham Seagull single-decker and the second one coming via Hardwicks in exchange for the 1963 Leyland PD3.

A revised red and more cream livery was introduced in July 1966 on Daimler/Roe MUB433 and MUM459 and these were joined by new HNW366D in November 1966. These three were the only ones in this revised livery.

Farsley also had visits by other demonstrators besides 327NMP, and the following were observed over the years:

- PTE592 in October 1954 and was a Leyland PSUC1/1 with Saro B44F body from June 1953. Whilst Ribble bought fifty, it also was on a loan to London Transport, without any sales.

- UJU774 was an AEC Reliance 2MU3RV with Willowbrook B45F body that came in March 1960, and was later sold to Gelligher.

- LYY827D came in July 1967 and was an AEC Swift MP2R with Marshall B48D body from 1966. The dual doors seen to have been liked as Farsley went on to order three Leyland Panthers with Alexander B48D bodies, but the order was cancelled before the Leeds take-over.

A photographic study of the fleet.

HL6368 was Farsley fleet number 6 and was a 1934 Leyland LT5A with Roe B32F body that came from West Riding in Wakefield in 1949. This and the next three buses were not used by WAT and HL6368 is seen in the old depot at Town Street, Stanningley with no nearside headlight, a starting handle and a watering can!

JUB356 is believed to be based on HL4742 from 1935 new to Bullocks, later West Riding and with a Burlingham body from 1945, the year of its re-registration. Notice the Jowett Bradford van alongside.

In the original fleet as No. 7 and new as a Daimler demonstrator in 1934, this COG5 with 1946 Roe B35F body was another of those not used by WAT. It is waiting in 1952 at the Old Ball terminus in Horsforth, with a dog behind, crossing the road.

Fleet No. 10 was GNW776, a 1938 Daimler that in 1948 got a new Roe body. It is at the depot in October 1952 alongside JUB356.

At the Old Ball terminus in original FOC livery is KUB695 that was fleet No. 8 and was one of four similar Daimler CVD6 with Roe B35F bodies. This one was new in March 1947 and stayed until 1961; much of its time with WAT on contract work.

Fleet No. 9 was LUB546 and like the other three single-deck Daimler CVD6s was new in March 1948. Now in the Wallace Arnold inspired livery it is in Town Street, Farsley.

In 1952 Farsley 11 is at Stanningley heading for Horsforth. Both 11 and 12 had this so called "streamlined livery" along with high back seats; thus they were the first choice vehicles for private hires. Farsley 11 has passed Bradford CT AEC Regent31 at the terminus of route 90 from Bradford – truly iconic buses with Weymann bodies and the subject of two books in this series "The Bradford to Queensbury bus, 1949 to 1974, part one, and part two".

In 1954, former No. 11 at the old depot in the WAT livery with their crest and the "Wallace Arnold Tours" name above the windows.

Former FOC fleet No. 12 in a reversed WAT livery. This 1948 bus stayed until 1957 when it returned to WAT and was rebodied with a Burlingham coach body from WAT KUM849 and then used by WAT for a few more years. It was replaced at Farsley by loaned MUB438.

HL8214 was one of three WAT coaches transferred in from October 1952 and replaced by four other WAT coaches in October 1954. (MUM275/458/460/461).

DUB926 had been bought by WAT for contract work in 1950. New in 1936 to Leeds Corporation Transport it came to Farsley from Hardwicks in 1954 and stayed until December 1956, being initially restricted to work from Pudsey to Rodley.

AUM404 was an AEC Regent O661 with MCCW body new 1935 to Leeds Corporation Transport and bought by WAT in December 1949 for contract work. It is seen here in April 1950 on football special work at Elland Road, Leeds. It went to the Hardwicks subsidiary from 1952 to 1954 and then returned to WAT Royston depot for contract work, before doing a few months' work with Farsley until its withdrawal in December 1956.

MUM461 with original Wilks and Meade coach body (as had MUM275/458 and 460) and seen with WAT in Blundell Street/Rigby Road, Blackpool. All four were used as such by Farsley from 1954, until they were all rebodied as double-deckers by Roe in 1956. MUM461 then stayed with FOC for a few years before being transferred across Leeds to Kippax.

The 1953 Plaxton body of 1950 NUA781, above, was fitted to LNW817 in 1953, and came to Farsley with similarly rebodied KUM837 & 849, all three having been originally bodied by Wilks and Meade like MUM275 above. These three came in October 1955 and stayed with FOC until February 1956 whilst MUM458/60/61 were being rebodied.

MUM458 is just delivered from Roe and shows the high rear step to enable the fitting of Roe's safety staircase, and not as has wrongly been noted by others, because of having a high chassis. Indeed, York Pullman's four new Roe-bodied AEC Regent IIIs in 1954/1955 also had the same high step. A former passenger recalls that "the rear entrance buses were well known for their strange bodywork on the platform which had a steep step on it before you reached the lower saloon".

WAT MUB437 and 438 were 1949 AEC Regals with unusual 1952 Bellhouse-Hartwell bodies that were at Farsley from December 1957 until June 1958 and had replaced the last two of the original Farsley Daimler single-deckers on the Tinshill route.

WAT RUG294 with Plaxton Venturer III body replaced one of MUB437/438 (shown on page 20) in 1958.

WAT YUM57 along with Plaxton-bodied RUG294, replaced one of MUB437/438 (shown on page 20) in 1958.

WAT MUB433 is a Daimler CVD6 that originally had a Wilks and Meade C33F body, then in 1954 a Plaxton FC33F body, and is seen here, when used by WAT on coach work. It was then rebodied by Roe as a double-decker and came to Farsley in January 1957 along with MUM459.

KUM849 in Pudsey BS in April 1966 and looking "weathered". Like MUM459 and MUB433 it is a Daimler CVD6 from 1949 and had a Wilks and Meade half cab C33F body that was replaced in 1954 with Plaxton FC33F bodies. Finally, it received a Roe H61R body in May 1957 and stayed until the end in 1968.

MUB433 was another Daimler with Wilkes & Meade then Plaxton body before being rebodied in 1957. It is seen here in the last livery in July 1966 at Pudsey Bus Station.

Former WAT Burlingham Seagull coach, WUM49 had bus seats fitted for work with Farsley. Identical WUM45 to 48 were also sent to the Hardwicks fleet in 1961. WUM45 is at Stanningley headed for Farsley and Rodley.

ARN185 was the spare bus for both the Farsley and Kippax fleets from 1958 to 1963 but was garaged at Farsley even though it was in Kippax livery. As the blind shows it did do some work whilst at Farsley.

909EUM was the first new 30 foot double-decker for Farsley in 1965 and was in 1967 exchanged for one of Hardwicks' Plaxton Panoramas, 9206NW, in 1967.

This dual purpose Plaxton 833KUA came in 1964 and was used by WAT on weekend excursion work. It was later painted in a reversed livery of cream with a red band and went to Hardwicks in 1968 after Farsley closed.

Former WAT 9206 and 9207NW are tucked up for the night. 9206NW came in 1967 from Hardwicks whilst 9207NW had replaced WUM49 in 1965. Both operated in full WAT livery until June 1967 when the red band livery was introduced. When Farsley closed, they both returned to WAT.

HNW366D was new in 1966 and, after the sale, was transferred to Hardwicks.

The End

On 31st March 1968, Wallace Arnold sold the company to Leeds Corporation, the owner Mr. Greenwood saying the operation was no longer covering its costs. The last day of working by Farsley vehicles was Saturday 30th March 1968. MUM459 was the last bus from Pudsey to the Old Ball and MUB433 worked the last service journey from Pudsey to Rodley, returning at 23.15 to Stanningley only.

MUB433 at Old Ball in Horsforth just before the close with "a man and a van" who is bringing a Leeds Corporation Transport bus stop, ready for the change.

The rear end of KUM849 leaving Pudsey Market Place".

Next day, Leeds City Transport introduced routes 79 (direct) and 80 (peak hours via Coal Hill Lane) as direct replacements from Pudsey to Horsforth (and on 9th September, both services went onto Tinshill following the rebuilding of the bridge). The basic frequency was 30 minutes Monday to Saturday and every hour on a Sunday.

Leeds initially used OMO AEC Swifts from the March 1968 batch 61 to 66 based at their Bramley depot, to which many Farsley staff had transferred. Bramley also provided at peak times, Leyland PD3As/Metro Cammell in the 324 to 330 series.

Leeds Corporation Transport 61 seen on 31st March 1968 in Pudsey Market Place on the first day of operation of route 79.

LCT329 at Bramley depot off a 79.

Kippax & District Motor Co. Ltd

The Route and History

The company was formed in 1924 as the Yellow Bus Service by the Watson Brothers and a Mr. Ridsdale (who later left). The buses had an over yellow livery with maroon relief and after the Second World War the livery was changed to maroon with three yellow bands.

They started a service in October 1925 from Leeds to Ledston Luck Colliery, via Cross Gates, Garforth and Kippax. Shortly afterwards a second service was introduced from Castleford to Church Fenton, travelling via Kippax, Garforth, Barwick and Aberford. This was, however, cut back in 1939 to Aberford, due to a decline in passenger traffic, and the frequency was gradually reduced until being finally abandoned in 1950.

The Leeds route from Ledston Luck was 11.42 miles long and had an hourly headway with a journey time of 39 minutes with the journey times:

- Ledston Luck to Kippax 4 minutes
- Kippax to Garforth 10 minutes
- Whitkirk 10 minutes
- Cross Gates 2 minutes
- Halton 2 minutes
- Leeds 11 minutes

On paper, a surprisingly relaxed timed route requiring two buses with layovers of 29 minutes in Leeds and 12 minutes at Ledston Luck, this allowing for delays along the busy roads and to provide an even hourly service. The first bus on the Ledston Luck route on Monday to Saturday was from Ledston Luck at 0709 hours and returned from Leeds at 0817 hours, with Sunday having a later start at 1309 hours. The last bus on every day from Ledston Luck to Leeds was at 2109 hours and this returned from Leeds at 2217 hours (or 2220 on Saturday) arriving at Ledston Luck at 2257/2300 hours from where it ran empty to the depot. Meanwhile, the second bus had left Leeds an hour earlier at 2117 hours and on arrival at Ledston Luck at 2148 hours it then left at 2209 hours for Kippax.

In the early 1950s contract services started from Kippax and Garforth to Burton's, the well-known clothing manufacturers in Leeds, and for a short time, football specials also ran to Leeds United's Elland Road ground.

On 1st June 1956 the company was bought by the Barr and Wallace Arnold Trust and continued as a subsidiary under the Kippax & District fleet name. Fleet numbers were discontinued, and the livery changed to be red with three yellow bands, this partially retaining the original Yellow Bus Service image.

On 4th September 1961 a new route started from Leeds to Ninelands in the Garforth area, running via the new housing Kingsway and Westbourne estates. With a distance of 8.49 miles taking 33 minutes, this route initially had three journeys in each of the morning and evening weekday peaks. Then in April 1962, an hourly Saturday service was started and required two buses, giving four buses per hour over the common route from Wakefield Road, Garforth to Leeds. There was no Sunday service to Ninelands.

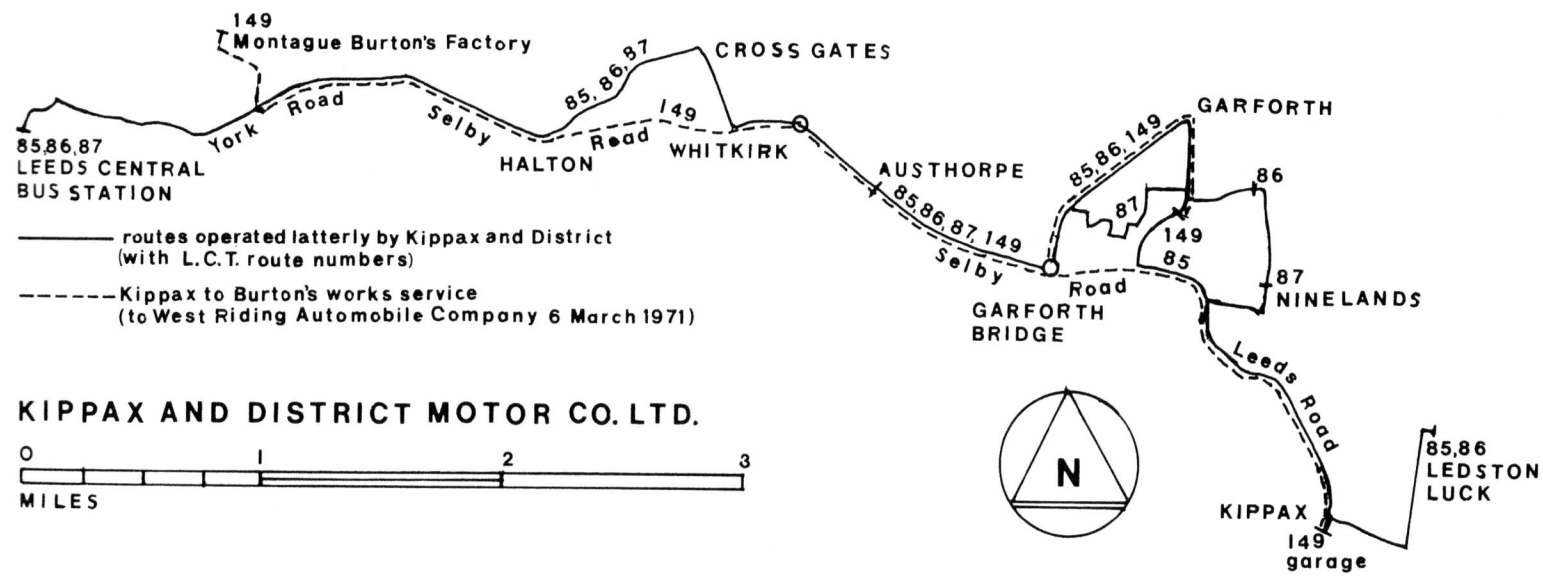

The routes are shown along with the subsequent Leeds CT route numbers. Route map courtesy of LTHS.

On 30th September 1963, Leeds Bus Station was remodelled and now instead of having stands at 90 degrees to York Street, the stands were now semi-curved. Originally, when opened in 1938, the width of the lanes was 18 foot wide for 7 foot 6 inch wide buses, now the lane's width was 24 feet. With five platforms of stands, the first three were for Leeds Corporation Transport and stands 4 and 5 were for the independents like Kippax, West Riding, Burrows and South Yorkshire.

The Fleet

A full fleet list is available on request, but the general fleet policy is covered here. Kippax & District always bought new vehicles and the fleet acquired in June 1956 was four double-deckers and two single-deckers.

Kippax & District outflank Burrows of Wombwell in the bus station. The K&D bus on the right is AWT128, an all-Leyland TD4 from 1935 and never came into the WAT stock as it was withdrawn in 1953. It had been the first double-decker and was replaced by the rebodied EWU247. GWX824 on the left came in 1948 and stayed until 1967. The Burrows was new in 1949 and went in 1966. So GWX wins the long service award by one year! Burrows' interesting operation is covered by another book in this series.

The two acquired single-deckers soon went by December 1956, and the four double-deckers were repainted by Wallace Arnold, losing their fleet numbers at the same time. The 1948 two all-Leyland PD2/1s became the mainstay of the fleet to 1967.

All-Leyland GWX824 in 1965 at the back of the former Leeds Corporation Transport bus repair works in Donisthorpe Street Leeds, a part of which was used by WAT for a short time. It has had some repairs, (note the new lower panelling) and more work is to follow.

In 1957 WAT transferred over two Daimler rebodied double-deckers that had formerly been coaches, and like the Farsley fleet, these Daimlers originally had their Wilks & Meade coach bodies replaced by bodies from other WAT coaches. One came on loan from the Farsley fleet, but this was eventually replaced by a permanently transferred Daimler/Roe from Farsley.

Then in June 1960 a new Leyland PD3 arrived; this was the first 30ft double-decker supplied to the Wallace Arnold subsidiaries. It had a revised red and yellow livery with black lower waist rail, which became the future standard. Another PD3 came in 1962 with the final two being delivered in 1965.

The two 1948 PD2s eventually went in early 1968 and were due to be replaced by two PD2s from Hardwicks. However, only one was suitable which entered service with Kippax in May 1967. The other Hardwicks PD2 had a cracked chassis, so this was replaced by the inevitable Daimler/Roe from Farsley.

So, when Kippax & District was bought by WAT in 1968 the fleet was the three Daimler/Roes, one all-Leyland PD2 and the four PD3/Roes.

Unlike Farsley, Kippax did not have many loans from WAT, although of course some did come. A Burlingham Seagull came for a short time in 1958 and the ex-Ribble PD1 also, being the spare for both Leeds fleets, showed up from time to time until it was scrapped in 1963. The WAT coach loans to Kippax seemed to be often for just one trip or a few days at most, although sometimes they stayed longer to cover vehicle overhauls. Their use was not always fully recorded.

Kippax also had two demonstrators visit:

- 327NMP a 1962 AEC Reliance 4MU3RA with Park Royal B54F body came in the middle of being trialled by Farsley, for three days in June 1962.
- KTD551C came for two weeks in June 1965 and was a Leyland Atlantean PDR1/1 with Park Royal H74F body. A successful visit, as two were ordered for 1968 delivery. These, however, were cancelled when the talks with Leeds Corporation Transport started. KTD however was eventually to stay in Yorkshire and was later bought by Woods of Mirfield.

Photographic study of the fleet.

No. 9 was BWR98 was an all-Leyland TD4, from 1936 and was kept on by WAT until December 1958.

Fleet No. 10 BWR147, was a 1937 AEC Regal 0662 with Roe B32F body and is in Leeds Bus Station, rather strangely showing Aberford via Barwick. The route actually ran from Castleford to Aberford and did not go into Leeds and was abandoned in 1950; perhaps it was just some "blind fiddling"? Like No. 11, it was quickly withdrawn six months after the WAT take-over. Two lowbridge West Riding double-deckers are on the flanks in the background.

Fleet No. 11 YG2465 was formerly No. 7 when it was a 1933 AEC Regal 662 with Duple coach body. It was rebodied by Roe as B32F in 1937 and was withdrawn six months after the WAT take-over.

Originally fleet No. 12 EWU247 was a Daimler CWA6 new in 1944 with a Roe UH56R body. In 1953 it was rebodied by Roe as seen here and looking new. It was then numbered 16 and worked on until September 1966. It was an early version of the Roe rebodied CVD6s that WAT "popularised" in their three stage bus fleets.

Nos. 14 and 15 were 1948 all-Leyland PD2s. They had a long life with Kippax until 1967. GWX823 in Leeds Bus Station is ready to leave for Garforth.

ASD121 was the first WAT purchase for Kippax and came from Western SMT in 1956. The 1943 Massey body was poor, so it was only in the fleet for a few months. It remained in Western livery until being scrapped by Blamires in Bradford.

WAT LNW869 with its original Wilks and Meade coach body that was replaced in 1952 with a Burlingham body from NUA752. Five years later it was rebodied as a double-decker in January 1957 by Roe and came to Kippax.

LNW869 Daimler/Roe came to Kippax in January 1957 and was there at the sale to Leeds Corporation Transport in 1968. It is waiting to move on stand in Leeds Bus Station and a West Riding all-Leyland lowbridge similarly waits behind.

ARN185, ex-Ribble in October 1958 and the spare bus for Kippax and Farsley (where it was garaged) is seen here showing a Farsley destination. It was scrapped in June 1963.

MUM461 was transferred from Farsley in March 1958 and is seen at Ledston Luck in June 1962, with the colliery in the background. Ledston Luck Colliery was sunk in the 1870s and was a few miles north of the larger mines in the Castleford area. Ledston Luck miners were the last to return to work in 1984-85 after the miners' strike. It closed two years later.

In June 1960 6237UB was the first 30 footer in the WAT stage bus fleets. Here it is in Leeds Bus Station with, in the background, the Quarry Hill Flats, designed in 1934 and noted for the size and modernist design. The flats had radical and modern features such as solid fuel ranges, electric lighting, a state-of-the-art refuse disposal system and communal facilities including a swimming pool. From 1938 Quarry Hill was the largest social housing complex in the UK, but, due to social problems and poor maintenance, the flats were demolished in 1978.

556DUA and EWU247 in August 1964 in Leeds Bus Station. EWU247 is a 1943 Daimler CWA6 with Roe UH56R body that was rebodied in 1953 by Roe and became No. 16. 556DUA was the second PD3/Roe and new in 1962.

From 1965, DUG166C is seen emerging into Selby Road at Halton in May 1966. After the sale to LCT it was sold on to Morgan (Blue Line) in Armthorpe, near Doncaster, for further service.

A Kippax DUG PD3 meets SUA296 a PD2 in Leeds Bus Station with a West Riding Wulfrunian behind. DUG167C was the last Kippax & District bus from Ledston Luck into Leeds and returned at 2310 hours to Kippax. SUA296 came from Hardwicks in May 1967 to replace GWX824 and was new in 1954.

The End

Wallace Arnold group sold the Kippax & District Motor Co. to Leeds Corporation Transport on 31st March 1968. The last day of operation was on Saturday 30th March 1968 and the five buses in service as follows:

- Ninelands with 6237UB and SUA296 (and the last bus on this service)
- Ledston Luck had MUM461 on duplicates from Kippax with 556DUA and DUG167C on the main service. The final journey was worked by DUG167C which ran the last Leeds departure to Kippax only, where it was boarded at Cross Hills, Kippax by all the remaining staff for the short journey to the depot.

The replacing Leeds routes on 31st March were:

- 85 Leeds to Ledston Luck; the main route
- 86 as above but with a diversion via Garforth Ninelands on weekday mornings and afternoons
- 87 Leeds to Garforth Ninelands
- 149 Works service from Kippax and Garforth to Burton's factory, Leeds

These were operated from Leeds Corporation's Torre Road No.1 depot on York Road using Regent Vs 949 to 968, coincidentally the same batch that were used on the former Ledgard routes from Leeds to Horsforth and Bradford that Leeds acquired, from West Yorkshire, in October 1967.

LCT952 elsewhere in Leeds at Shadwell.

None of the Kippax staff joined Leeds Corporation Transport as the route was now being worked from the opposite end, plus, LCT had no need for part-time staff, yet Kippax had employed six conductresses on that basis.